Aspects to Horoscope Angles

Vivia Jayne

Copyright 1975 by Vivia Jayne

All rights reserved.

No part of this book may be reproduced or transmitted in any form or by any means, electronic or mechanical, including photocopying or recording, or by any information storage and retrieval system, without written permission from the author and publisher. Requests and inquiries may be mailed to: American Federation of Astrologers, 6535 S. Rural Road, Tempe AZ 85283.

ISBN-10: 0-86690-551-0
ISBN-13: 978-0-86690-551-0

First Printing: 1975
Current Printing: 2014

Cover Design: Jack Cipolla

Published by:
American Federation of Astrologers, Inc.
6535 S. Rural Road
Tempe AZ 85283

www.astrologers.com

Printed in the United States of America

Contents

Preface	v
Aspects to the Horoscope Angles in Radical Charts	1
The Three Local Planes: Midheaven, Ascendant, and Vertex	5
Delineations of Lights and Planets to Angles	9
Aspects of Planets and Lights to the Midheaven and their Meanings	11
Aspects of Planets and Lights to the Ascendant and their Meanings	17
Examples	23
Chart Data	73

Preface

There is very little material in the literature on astrology concerning aspects to the angles, i.e. the Ascendant, Midheaven and Vertex. The main reason for this is that only a few astrologers have had an extensive experience in correcting the time of birth (rectification). Vivia Jayne, who has studied astrology for a quarter of a century, has been rectifying horoscopes for the past 20 years.

Other things being equal, the most important factors in a horoscope are the Lights (Sun and Moon) and the three angles. The importance of aspects to the Lights and between them is widely recognized, but the aspects to the angles are equally vital. The widespread failure to use such aspects is one of the most glaring faults in modern astrology. Careful study of this book will enable astrologers at all levels of competence to correct this deficiency. Mrs. Jayne's work has forced me to revise some of my own ideas as to the significance of the hard aspects to the angles. She found, after studying many cases (only a few are given in the book), that even squares and oppositions have strongly beneficent effects despite the problems also shown by them.

Some light on this subject has also been cast by the brilliant Ken Gillman in a most valuable article in *Kosmos* (Volume VI, #2, 1974, pp.78-99), "Researching Aspects." Drawing his conclusions directly from the data—600 cases—he avoids the bias imposed by theory and tradition. The results are surprising and appear to be significant. A lower square of the Sun to the Ascendant, for instance, is stronger and quite different from an upper square (Sun in the third or fourth house as contrasted with the ninth or tenth). His work underlines the importance of aspects to the angles and suggests that we must avoid a doctrinaire approach. Unfortunately, he does not tell us about the estimated accuracy of his birth times, which has a most direct bearing on his conclusions.

In the back of this book a list will be found that provides the given time, the rectified time and the person(s) who did the rectification on all the charts discussed in the book. Since most of the charts were rectified by either Mrs. Jayne and me or me, she has had plenty of opportunity to observe how accurate the rectification was under later aspects by direction. Only those charts which passed this test have been chosen by her. One chart was rectified by Miss Eleanore Hesseltine, the top rectifier we have known, and one by Johndro (his own chart). Since the reliability of the conclusions of this book hang on accurate birth times, Mrs. Jayne has made a special effort to be sure of their accuracy.

Charles A. Jayne
October 1974

Aspects to the Horoscope Angles in Radical Charts

There is no easy way to answer such questions as: "What does a person do for a living?" "How many brothers and sisters does a person have?" or some of the other seemingly simple questions people ask about a horoscope or a given individual. It is particularly difficult to answer such questions if the astrologer doesn't know the person and is just given a "cold" chart and asked these questions or told to interpret and give a picture of the individual's life. I know there are astrologers who believe that there is some simple one-to-one correlation that can give you an instant answer to very literal questions. I am not one of them. I have found that in order to be sure of your ground, especially when interpreting the horoscope of someone you have never met, it is essential to analyze the total chart before drawing any conclusions.

This book is intended to be helpful in giving you one more tool to use in interpreting a horoscope, especially when it comes to the understanding of planetary aspects to the angles. Most astrologers are familiar with the importance of planets rising near the Ascendant and their effect on the personality. Yet they are not equally aware of the importance of the effect other aspects, such as squares, semisquares, sextiles, quincunxes, trines, oppositions, sesquiquadrates, parallels, and contraparallels, of the planets and Lights to the angles. This is especially true when it comes to the Midheaven's aspects; such aspects can be enormously helpful in telling you what kind of career and/or reputation a person has. Aspects to the Ascendant are, of course, more personal in meaning.

Although I have given a list on the following pages of what each planet and the Lights to the angles mean, the interpretation should not be taken too literally. This can be understood when one realizes that the sign the planet or Light is in, the house it rules, the house it aspects from, the sign the Midheaven, Vertex or Ascendant is in, all have to be taken into consideration. For this reason I decided to make this a workbook where actual horoscopes are used and interpreted in order to give you a move specific method of using planets and Lights to angles. The material here is not meant to be a complete book on interpreting a horoscope. For those of you just beginning to learn how to interpret a chart, I would refer you to one of the many textbooks on horoscope interpretation. The emphasis here will be mostly stressing aspects to angles, but of course in the charts I use I will have to delineate much of the chart in order to get a more accurate interpretation of each aspect.

It is assumed that the reader has some elementary knowledge of the rectification of a horoscope; at least what I call the "common sense" rectification of the angles should be understood. When a person gives you the time of a horoscope to the nearest 15 minutes, you may assume that the time of birth could be off a bit. If, when you set up the chart, you discover the Ascendant to be late in a sign, let us say Cancer, you know that the time of the horoscope could be inaccurate enough to make either Cancer or Leo the Ascendant. You should be able to decide by carefully questioning the person whether he or she has a Cancer or Leo

Ascendant, whether the planets fall in the right houses and, as we shall see later, whether the planetary aspects to the angles all fit the pattern of the life and personality.

I have found that planetary aspects to the Ascendant can greatly modify the personality projection of the particular sign there. For instance, while Neptune was traveling through Leo there were many people born with Neptune in Leo rising. Neptune seems to considerably alter Leo's usually direct and open approach to things, adding a touch of reclusiveness and shyness and a good deal of fey subtlety. Of course, the planet has to be close enough to the exact degree rising in order to have this effect. Actually it isn't only the planet rising that modifies the Ascendant, as just mentioned. Squares, sextiles, trines, oppositions, parallels, sesquiquadrates, and contraparallels of planets or Lights to the Ascendant or Midheaven all have an effect and should be considered when rectifying a chart. This kind of "common sense" rectification anyone can do without getting into the more complicated mathematical calculations which follow when trying to get the chart pinned down to the exact minute of birth.

In some of the case histories to follow I give examples of people who came to see me who had a certain sign and degree on the Ascendant. After asking specific questions and by using planetary aspects to the Midheaven and Ascendant, I was able to decide which was the approximately right degree to have on the Midheaven and on the Ascendant. Of course, for exact rectification of the horoscope you have to test directions to the angles and compare them with exact events of the past life to be sure you have the angles "set" to the minute.

The orbs I use between planets and angles are the same orb I use between planets in a horoscope. I use a seven degree orb on either side of exactitude for the Sun and Moon to angles, and a five degree orb on either side of exactitude for the planets to angles. These orbs are the ones I use for the major aspects such as squares, oppositions, conjunctions, parallels, and contraparallels. I use slightly smaller orbs for trines to the angles: five degrees for Lights, and four degrees for planets. I should say here that although weaker aspects such as sextiles, semisquares, sesquiquadrates, and quincunxes really do have an affect on the personality projection (Ascendant), or lend further description to the career or reputation (Midheaven), the orbs should be close to exact (within one degree). Of course in cases where you have T-Cross configurations of many planets involved with angles you sometimes have to allow wider orbs. This is true because the closer planets pull the wider planets into orb by being conjunction, opposition, trine, or square to each other as well as contacting the angles. This will also be brought up in some of the cases I use. Students have asked me many times just exactly how a planetary aspect works if it's a wide orb and whether you can interpret it the same way as tightly-knit bodies. I always say a thing is what it is (a la Jones). If an aspect of a planet to an angle or a Light to an angle is wide, then its action in the life will probably be intermittent and not very powerful. If it is a very close tight aspect involved with an angle, it is almost continuously active and noticeable in the life pattern of the person.

I would be remiss if I did not mention planetary pictures involving the angles. Hans Niggeman, who is an authority on Uranian astrology, says, "Planetary pictures are a grouping of two or more factors symmetrically placed around a common axis." Obviously if this "common axis" is the Midheaven, Ascendant, or Vertex, it is a very important feature of any horoscope and should be carefully looked for. There also can be indirect planetary pictures where an angle is square, semisquare, or sesquiquadrate to the axis of symmetry. Examples will also be shown using these.

The Three Local Planes: Midheaven, Ascendant, and Vertex

Ascendant

The horizon is the most obvious one of the three local planes. When the Sun crosses this point at sunrise it is at the Ascendant. The opposite point, or when the Sun sets or goes beneath the horizon, is the Descendant. The Ascendant is the cusp of the first house.

In a horoscope, aspects to the Ascendant degree are the significant ones used. It is the first thing you see when meeting a person. The kind of personality or facade that is projected is indicated by the Ascendant, the sign it is in, the planets and Lights aspecting it, and the ruler of the Ascendant sign. It also shows the kind of people you will attract to your doorstep and your manner of dealing with people in a tete-a-tete way.

Midheaven

The second of the three local planes is at a right angle to the horizon and is called the Meridian. The Sun crosses this Meridian at True Local Noon and is then at the Midheaven. In the northern temperate zone the Sun is somewhat south at noon.

The opposite point is the Imum Coeli, or bottom of the sky; the Sun crosses this point of the Meridian at midnight. In the northern temperate zone the Sun is somewhat north at midnight.

The Midheaven is the cusp of the tenth house for most house systems and generally reveals the person's standing and reputation in his world. The profession, career, business and/or ambitions are shown by this point. Of course, the entire tenth house and its contents should be studied for a complete delineation of the above. Even though Jupiter is in the tenth house but not close enough to the Midheaven degree to make an aspect, it has an effect on the career and reputation.

The parents are also described by this vertical axis (Midheaven-Imum Coeli, running south to north). It seems accurate to use the Midheaven and contents of the tenth house as at least partially representing the most influential parent. The IC, or cusp of the fourth house, and the contents of the fourth house represent the less influential parent. Also, planets and Lights in the horoscope show the parents, such as the Sun-Saturn for father and the Moon-Pluto for mother. Their circumstances at birth are shown by the Midheaven-IC axis.

Vertex

The Prime Vertical is the third local plane running east and west at right angles to both the Horizon and the Meridian. When the Sun crosses the west wall (Prime Vertical) and is due west, it is at the Vertex; sometimes this is below the Horizon and sometimes it is above it. It is at the Anti-Vertex, when it crosses the east wall (Prime Vertical) and is due east. The Sun moves in the ecliptic plane so that the three angles are formed by its intersection with each of the three local planes.

In this book you will not find as many examples using the Vertex as you do the other two angles since it is still under study and there is much yet to be discovered about it. It appears to be a very "fateful" angle in the chart, one over which we have little control and involves us with group karma in some way. It is the least personal and least conscious of the three angles.

Delineation of Lights and Planets to Angles

The delineations of planets and Lights to the angles in succeeding chapters should not be used verbatim and applied to any particular horoscope. They are simply meant to be used as guidelines to be mixed with all the other aspects to the angles in order to get a more accurate picture of the individual.

For instance, if you are looking at a horoscope that has Neptune conjunction Ascendant, it would be inaccurate to simply look at the delineation for Neptune-Ascendant to get a description of the personality. You would first need to note the sign rising.

Let us suppose in this case the sign is Leo. You would then take note of any other longitudinal aspects to the Ascendant. In our hypothetical case we will say the Jupiter is square the Ascendant and the Sun is sextile it. Check also for declination aspects. Here we have Mercury contraparallel Ascendant. Now, an aspect has two ends, unless it is a parallel or conjunction. In this case we are looking for a description of the outer personality, so we look especially at the end affecting the Ascendant.

If you wish to find the circumstances that are affected in the life you will pay special attention to the house and sign that the planet aspects from. In this case of Jupiter square Ascendant, the Jupiter is in the fourth house in Leo, which has a special meaning relating to home, roots and family.

But the important point personality-wise is that Jupiter aspects a Leo Ascendant along with Neptune, Sun, and Mercury. Mixing all these influences together we would have to say that the person has an open, frank, cheerfully sunny (Leo) and naively (Neptune) sympathetic (Jupiter) personality with a gift for gab (Mercury) and getting ideas across (Mercury). This pretty much describes the impression one gets on first meeting. To go deeper into the character and life pattern you naturally must go further into the horoscope and its meaning.

Aspects of Planets and Lights to the Midheaven and Their Meanings

Sun

The Sun in any aspect to the Midheaven brings the person into touch with authorities, the government, honorable and affluent people and positions. Even when the aspect is a difficult one, the influence still brings some good fortune and has a benign influence on the career, family, and reputation. Among the sample charts there are several leaders and presidents of countries, all of whom have aspects of the Sun to Midheaven, some of them stressful aspects.

A man or men are usually helpful to the career and may boost the reputation. While the afflicting Sun-Midheaven aspects usually present problems both circumstantial and psychological, they still introduce higher positions of authority and good fortune. I consider the Sun to the angles to be the most benign contact possible in a horoscope.

Moon

The Moon also has a fortunate effect when aspecting the Midheaven. But while the Sun puts the person in touch with high people and positions, the Moon emphasizes public recognition and being known by the masses.

In career and business, the person deals with the public and may receive much publicity. This can be accompanied by problems and/or conflict, depending upon whether the aspect is stressful or not. The Moon also has to do with women who may figure largely in the person's career activities or have an important influence on one's reputation, standing, and ambitions.

Mercury

Mercury almost always indicates that the person will deal with words in business or professional interests. This may be public speaking, writing, or even message carrying.

Of course, everyone who has Mercury-Midheaven aspects is not necessarily a professional writer or speaker, but you can be sure that one of the two fits largely into whatever business or professional interests one has. These people will be publicly known as speakers or writers even though their profession may be that of president, media personality, or mail-carrier. It enables them to bring words (Mercury) to the public (Midheaven).

Where the aspect is an affliction, they may dislike what they are doing or have problems getting their ideas across, but they seem propelled in this direction anyway.

Venus

Venus is the planet of adornment, beauty, sociability, and gratification, so one can expect those with this planet contacting the Midheaven to have a reputation for charm and affability.

They may be in careers involving beauty such as interior decoration, hairstyling, makeup artist, or modeling. They are usually excellent at giving or promoting public social functions and are good sales people. Women noted for their beauty often have Venus-Midheaven contacts. Actors whose looks are very important to their careers often have this contact. Marilyn Monroe, for example, had Venus conjunct the Midheaven.

The Venus-Midheaven person usually looks for emotional satisfaction in his or her business activities. If the contact is an affliction, there is often much drive to gratify oneself through the profession and perhaps the person never really feels completely satisfied with results. Venus-Midheaven is an excellent contact for the artist.

Mars

Aspects of Mars to the Midheaven give us people whose business interests involve machinery, soldiers, decision-making executive types, athletes, and enforcers of the law—people who would never be satisfied with quiet, sit-down careers. They may have a reputation for being quick and first in business affairs, and are willing to do things alone.

In affliction the same is true but they may have to expend a great deal of energy to reach their goals. They usually have a lot of drive and often reach the top through sheer aggressive push and one-pointedness. Starting new ventures is their cup of tea but they are not always so good when it comes to the patience needed to finish business projects unless aspects from other planets help out. They are not averse to a good fight and at some time in the life may be involved in a public controversy of no small proportions.

Jupiter

Jupiter aspects with the Midheaven are much like the Sun in that they usually bring prominent people into the life. Those with special honors or good family "names" may have this contact. It also seems to have something to do with conventional religious interests and publishing. Even if the person does not have special high-ranking family backing, he or she is brought into contact with such people through interests outside the home.

Bankers, lawyers, and professional people in general seem often to have this aspect. Large and expansive businesses are described by Jupiter-Midheaven contacts and people who work for very large and wealthy organizations may have this configuration. They usually have a reputation for being honorable and respected citizens.

Saturn

Saturn in aspect to the Midheaven degree usually shows one who has much responsibility and discipline connected with his or her career. When the person is young, it seems to describe the father or some older male image rather than the person's profession. It refers to any business where there is much detail and hard work involved. Carefulness and a mature sense of one's obligations go with this position. Doctors often have this as one of the important contacts to their Midheaven. The person will have a reputation for being steady, reliable, and conservative.

Traditionally, Saturn was supposed to indicate a downfall at some time in the person's life. Yet I seem to find that this so-called "downfall" only occurs when the individual turns his or her back on responsibilities which rest on his or her shoulders. This is one thing a Saturn-Midheaven type can't seem to get away with.

Uranus

People in freelance jobs or careers that involve much change, variety, and travel usually have this contact to the Midheaven. Depending upon other aspects to Uranus, it can mean many changes and ups and downs in business and outside-the-home activities. Interests connected with aeronautics or electricity can also be shown.

These people often work under much tension with very irregular schedules which demand that they be ready at a moment's notice. The unusual, different, and new, or avant garde accompanies their professional affairs. Also, they may have a reputation for being eccentric or unusual and independent in their career activities.

Neptune

Neptune is associated with careers involving much creativity, the occult, and/or predicting the future. All the creative fields such as music, art, writing, and poetry seem doubly enhanced when Neptune adds its contact to the Midheaven angle. There may be something hidden or confidential in what they do and often it indicates that much of their career activity is carried on when alone or behind the scenes.

If other aspects assist, they may be helping humanity in some way or be connected with hospitals and/or retreats. There seem to be many artists and astrologers with this configuration. There are also social workers with this aspect. People who deal with make-believe, such as actors, makeup or film experts, or stage set designers and decorators have Neptune in aspect to the Midheaven.

Pluto

Pluto indicates primarily that some woman in the life has a powerful influence over the individual's career and ambitions. Detectives, research workers, and people who delve beneath the surface for hidden motives will often have this planet stimulating the Midheaven. Psychiatrists, psychological professions of all kinds, and those connected with products beneath the earth, such as oil, may have this contact.

When Pluto is involved with other planets, such as Venus, it can indicate one who deals with female sexual glamor in the career. Pluto-Mars-Midheaven can show jazz musicians. Even when the career does not fall under one of these headings, psychological insight and shrewdness are talents these people apply to business.

Aspects of Planets and Lights to the Ascendant and Their Meanings

Sun

The Sun in aspect to the Ascendant gives the personality added stature. In a woman's chart it usually indicates that there is an important male figure always in the life who has a strong beneficent effect on her personally.

If the Sun is within orb (seven degrees) of a conjunction to the Ascendant, the individual's personality projection is very powerful and he or she comes on very strong. It is hard to notice other people in the room when there is an angular Sun person there.

The Sun in aspect to the Ascendant is certainly one of the most beneficial contacts a horoscope can have and especially insofar as it effects personal relationships and overall success throughout the lifetime. These people can almost get by on personality alone. Even when the aspect is a so-called difficult one, the overall effect is still favorable and brings some degree of affluence and honor into the life.

Moon

The Moon contacting the Ascendant brings the individual into contact with many people in a personal way. They deal with people face-to-face as a part of their everyday life. It can also make them moody and somewhat fluctuating in temperament. There is more sentiment and emotions are more apparent to the observer.

The Moon being feminine, women or women's interests can play an important part in the personal life.

Unless the Moon is badly afflicted, aspects of Moon to Ascendant are definitely benefic. It brings opportunity by way of many personal contacts that can be described as a kind of popularity.

Mercury

The Mercury-Ascendant person is something of a talker. In fact, it is hard for these people to remain silent. They have a way with words and can be very witty, depending on the other planets contacting Mercury and the Ascendant. In any case their minds project actively.

Mercury is a highly sensitive planet, rather chameleon-like, and perceptive; the individual is likely to project these qualities in his or her personality. They have quick-moving eyes, very seldom miss anything, and display a restless quality that is singularly mercurial in nature.

Naturally the above qualities are modified by the closeness of the aspect and the sign rising. They have a curiosity that can sometimes get them into hot water.

Venus

Venus in aspect to the Ascendant certainly adds much natural graciousness and charm to the personality. If not actually beautiful or handsome, these people are certainly more attractive than the average person. Their good looks can gain them much attention and they may often be spoiled with pampering and petting as children.

As they grow older the influence usually matures into a more refined and hospitable manner. But it can show the negative side, be vain and self-centered. If the personality remains undeveloped, there can be a craving for attention and a kind of narcissism.

Mars

Mars to the Ascendant makes the person more aggressive and disputatious than he or she ordinarily would be. These people seem to attract more violence, either physical or mental. If Mars aspects the Ascendant by declination, and especially from a cadent house, it usually is psychological or mental aggressiveness.

These people like to be first, have a naturally competitive approach to things and love to give orders like a first sergeant. If the rest of the chart agrees, they are not averse to a few curse words and can resort to crudeness on occasion.

In a woman's horoscope this aspect usually means that there are very few periods in the life when she is without a man.

Jupiter

Jupiter aspecting the Ascendant adds a positivity to the personality that the individual shows to the world. The manner is confident, bouncy, and full of breeziness. Jupiter has protective qualities and along with an expansive attitude the person can be just plain lucky at times. They are saved from trouble just in the nick of time.

There is an openness aid frankness about their countenance that is reminiscent of Sagittarius on the Ascendant. Fortunate people may be attracted to their doorstep because of this influence. They seem constantly to expect the best of things—at least they appear that way on the surface.

If Jupiter is afflicted by Neptune, Mars, or Venus, and even the Sun, the effects are still fortunate but they may tend to expand in too many directions or to bite off more than they can chew or need.

Saturn

Saturn contacting the Ascendant is a much more inhibiting influence and can make the person appear very serious and older than he or she really is. Sometimes it makes the individual seem shy and retiring even though the rest of the horoscope may indicate that he or she is accomplished and sure-footed.

If Saturn is very close to the degree rising, there can be trouble at birth; sometimes the baby is what is known as a "blue baby."

These people are usually hard-working and unless Saturn is very badly afflicted can accept responsibility with ease. They can have an impressive appearance and manner, being the strong, silent type. But this is the mature side of Saturn, and usually the stranger first meeting him or her may think the person cold or indifferent. This attitude is just a defensive cover for the natural first reserve on meeting people.

The undeveloped type can be downright cheap, not only with others but with themselves. Duty and discipline are their first names.

Uranus

Uranus aspecting the Ascendant usually makes the person taller, depending upon the sign and other aspects the Ascendant has. It makes for a rather restless, unpredictable personality. Sudden changes in direction or mood can be very disconcerting while their manner can be aloof, eccentric or cool at varying times. They outwardly appear to be independent, although just the opposite may be the case when you get to know them.

These people attract unusual, even brilliant, people and are inclined to be willful. They are not especially cooperative and take delight in adopting the opposite stand from that which is popular or asked for.

They are difficult people to get close to. Close relationships don't usually last with them unless the two people agree to unusual mutual independence.

Neptune

Neptune contacts to the Ascendant give the personality a more receptive and sensitive quality. In fact, these people may "pick up" all kinds of surrounding impressions, some of which can make them feel uncomfortable.

There is a reclusive tendency, the person having an instinct to withdraw into privacy. Of course this is modified depending on the sign the Ascendant is in.

The emotions are more active and closer to the surface. They usually project an air of democratic sympathy and are often inclined to mimic the person they are with or pretend to be something they are not which is probably why they can make fine actors or actresses. There is an intangible, fey-like quality that leaves an elusive impression on others.

Because of their manner and subtlety they are difficult to understand or pin down. This contact can attract what I call "leaners" or dependent types and can also make the person dependent on others.

Pluto

These people are usually very shrewd and psychologically acute. While appearing to be mild-mannered and without direction, they almost always know exactly what they want, where they are going (no matter how indirectly) and how they are going to get there. They have a knack for seeing through anything phony and being able to understand the inner motives of others.

Their relationships with others have a strong element of psychological need that works both ways. And they are not above using others' weaknesses or needs to their advantage when necessary. There is a sexual quality about their demeanor or glance. They are inclined to be more secretive, laconic, and less talkative with these aspects. On the negative side, they can become too suspicious of others and develop an overly defensive manner.

Example One

This is the horoscope of a long-time client who, among other things, is an antique dealer. This, I think, is shown by Saturn sextile the Midheaven and Venus trine it. The sextile of Saturn is wide but Venus pulls the aspect in by being sextile Saturn as well as trine the Midheaven. You will note that Venus rules the fourth house, and this man has also made a sideline career out of buying and selling real estate.

Venus is a very focal body here since it aspects both the Midheaven and the Ascendant. Its position is on what Dr. Davidson used to call the "hidden" side of the seventh house cusp. This usually means the person has a private alliance (silent partner, if you will) who is of great importance to the native. This certainly is true of this man who has a personal as well as business associate who virtually runs his antique shop, does a lot of the strenuous jobs and is also a personal companion.

My client's health is under par, and he had one lung removed. His health problem has been one of the major things in his life, shown by a sixth house Sun in Gemini square to Saturn in the eighth. His "silent partner" is almost indispensable to him for health reasons. Because his Sun, pulled in by Mercury, is quincunx the Midheaven, and Jupiter and Saturn are trine his

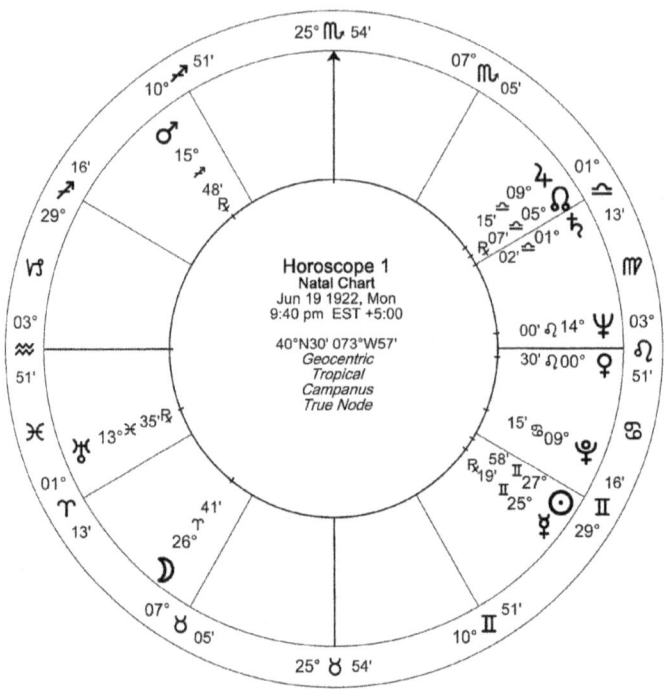

Ascendant, he has been able to get financial help from the government (Sun). His lung problem started when he was in the army and was injured in battle.

His vitality is not great, yet he has been able to build his business activities to a fairly successful level because of the kindness and help of his partner. He has the Midheaven at the midpoint of his second house Moon and sixth house Sun—both having a benign influence on career.

One should also notice that Pluto is contraparallel the Ascendant. When he did not seem to recover from surgery the way he should, he was sent to a psychiatrist, whose care he was under for some time to determine whether part of his health problems were not psychosomatic. The treatment did little good however, and they wound up diagnosing his problem as coming from a pinched nerve in the absent lung area.

Example Two

This horoscope is a good example of how much you could miss about the career and reputation if you were not using aspects to angles.

This woman has traveled a great deal and in connection with her career. She has been to Europe under the auspices of a large foundation (Moon conjunction Midheaven from the ninth house and Jupiter sextile the Midheaven from the eleventh ruling altruistic groups or foundations) in order to collect and do research (Pluto trine the Midheaven) on educational and culturally oriented books (ninth house). On the face of it you would wonder how she could ever travel comfortably and without mishap since the Mercury-Moon opposes Neptune from the ninth house. One might say that she would not do well in ninth house matters even though the Mercury-Moon opposite Neptune is resolved by the Mars-Saturn opposition. (The latter is a harsh aspect involving unsympathetic planets and is only very slightly helpful to the opposition of Moon-Neptune).

Just the reverse is true. She has met extremely important, affluent and unusually prominent people (Sun-Moon conjunction to the Midheaven, Sun-Moon midpoint exactly on the

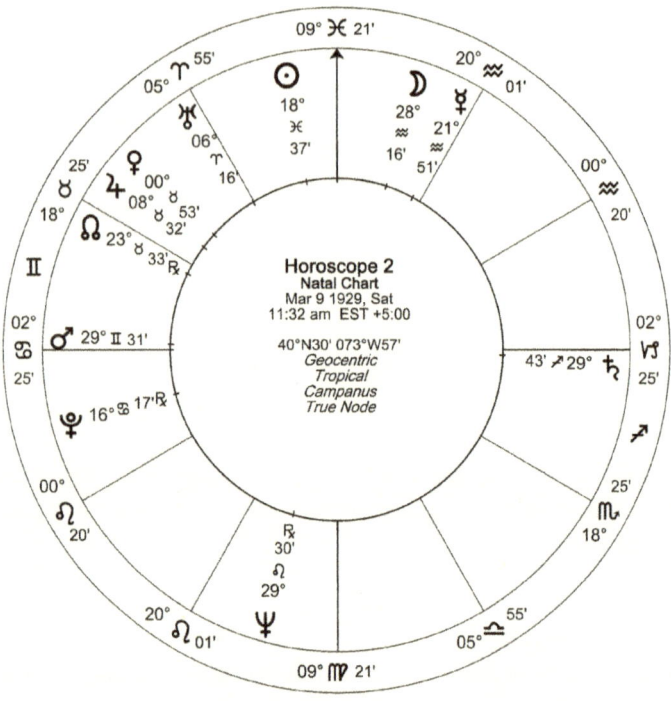

Midheaven, and Jupiter sextile the Midheaven) who have been very beneficial to her career and education, as well as spiritually enlightening. This, in spite of the fact that her family beginning is not all that solid or fortunate. After all, the Moon is ruler of the chart (rules Ascendant) and would be a very important influence in the life. This is a perfect example of how benefic the two lights can be to the angles and how they tend to elevate conditions in the individual's life.

She has a soft watery quality (Cancer Ascendant with Neptune, Moon, Venus aspecting it) with a good deal of graciousness and subtle charm. Yet she projects a severe self-disciplined quality, too, making you know that she is a "no-nonsense" type (Mars conjunction Ascendant, Saturn opposing it). She has had cooperative relationships and one private alliance with older men, both of whom had health problems and to whom she was very helpful (Neptune opposition Moon configuration helping the Mars-Ascendant-Saturn configuration).

She is now a member of a religious group where she is again being helpful to the leader of the group who is a most remarkable man, another example of how this Jupiter-Sun-Moon-Midheaven pattern works in her life. She is again being helpful in health matters, too (Pluto ruling sixth trine Midheaven) and is closely cooperative with an older man in a personal way (Mars-Saturn-Ascendant).

She is a craftswoman who has had a background in the arts and weaving (Venus sextile Ascendant) and has been able to be helpful to the group's activities through this medium. The secret alliance with a man of some years was equivalent to a secret marriage (shown by Saturn opposing the Ascendant on the "hidden side" of the Descendant).

Example Three

This is the chart of a physician born into a family of above-average comfort and advantages. He is educated well, received his M.D., and went on to earn certification in psychiatry.

Here again the Angles are extremely important keynotes to the career and personality, and he has not really been as successful as one would assume he should be.

His Midheaven has only a sextile of Sun and a very wide conjunction of Moon—the two most important contacts for impact on the world around you. He also has Saturn square his Midheaven and conjunction the Ascendant. This shows both in his great self-discipline and self-control (Saturn-Ascendant) and his conflict about being tied down with professional responsibilities (Saturn square Midheaven), and at the same time being offered positions of responsibility.

Mars trine Midheaven gives him a natural administrative ability. Being a psychiatrist is shown by Pluto opposition Midheaven (Pluto ruling psychological interests) and Moon conjunction Midheaven (dealing with the public professionally). The Sun sextile the Midheaven has brought him help from be-

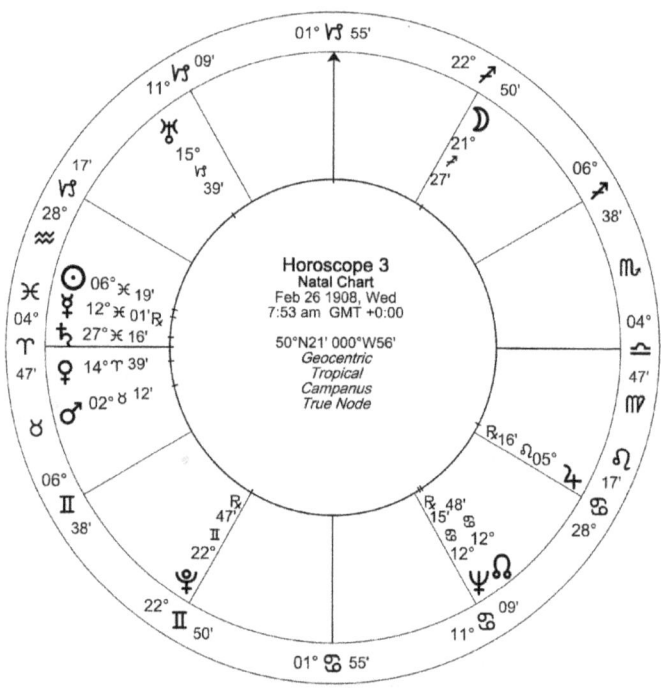

hind the scenes and through special work in hospitals (twelfth house). Nevertheless he would have done much better had he been born with "stronger" aspects of the lights to his Midheaven.

He would be more successful in an administrative position where accurate decisions and initiative are important (Mars trine Midheaven). There have been numerous opportunities of this kind in his life, but to some extent he has held himself back (Mars rules his Ascendant) from these involvements for fear (Saturn square Midheaven) of being burdened by too much responsibility that would curtail his love of travel and "getting around." Venus rising is square Uranus and Neptune, giving restlessness and a taste for variety. Moon in the ninth house also shows travel.

His personality is breezy (Jupiter) and positive (Aries) but alternately serious, reserved, and conventional (Saturn). He sometimes seems to vacillate or be strangely sensitive and emotional (Neptune-Ascendant). He can be very suave and ingratiating with Venus rising in the first house—a complex personality projection, but indeed fascinating.

He has had far above average vitality and health with Jupiter trine his Ascendant. Also, people who work for him or who might be considered his inferiors have been most obliging and helpful to him in personal ways. Neptune square the Ascendant from the fifth house seems to describe his sentimental and emotional attitude and feelings towards his only child, who has been some cause for anxiety and disturbance in his life.

Example Four

This is the chart of a woman who was thrown out into the world on her own early in life (Uranus opposition Midheaven). There have been many ups and downs in her career but she has been quite successful in business and in dealing with important men in authoritative positions (Sun trine Midheaven).

The Neptune conjunction Cancer Midheaven has enabled her to foresee into the future about what the public will want. Since this was very important to her job as a buyer, she impressed her superior with this ability and was able to make money at it too (Sun is on the hidden side of the second house).

Neptune is not overly fond of hard work and would much prefer to do things the easy way. This she has been able to do to some extent when it comes to making money. She even traded in the stock market on a daily basis which enabled her to make a profit without making any capital investment. The positions she held were hectic (Uranus) and she made a number of changes over the years and also traveled in connection with her career.

She has a strong personality projection and is capable of selling you the proverbial "Brooklyn Bridge." Her sales ability is ad-

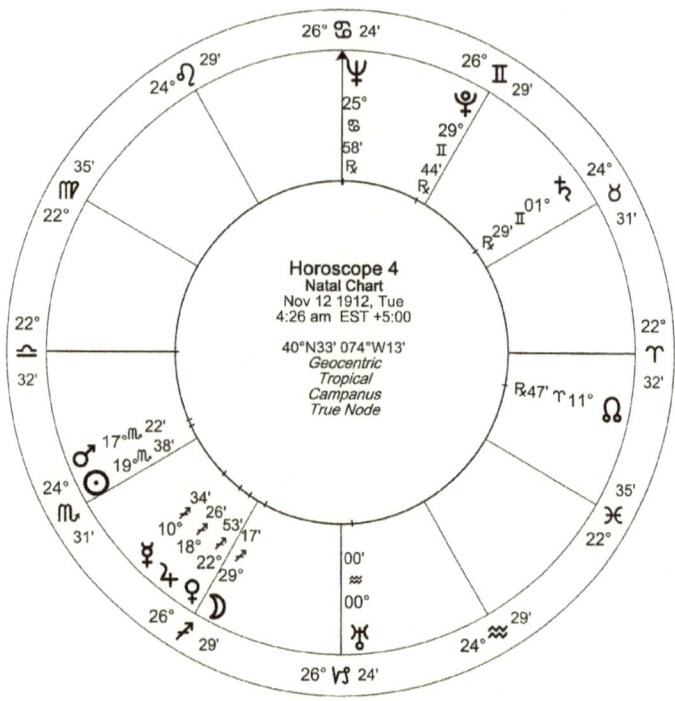

equately shown by Mercury semisquare Ascendant (gift of gab) and Venus sextile Libra Ascendant (cajoler). She attempts to persuade, talk, and charm you to her way of thinking and doing.

The Mars, of course, is late in the first but still gives an extra dash of aggressiveness to the personality. She dresses in a very ornate way with much jewelry and makeup (Jupiter and Venus sextile Ascendant). While she appears to be most agreeable and a "yes" girl on the surface (Libra), she has a will or iron underneath (Scorpio Mars and Sun).

The Pluto trine her Ascendant has made her a very shrewd judge of people and how to handle them. She has a natural psychological insight into what makes people tick.

Something should also be said about her Sun opposition the Vertex at 24 Taurus 19. Not only has she been very much involved with important businessmen (Sun trine Midheaven) but she has also had to deal with key people without whom the organization probably wouldn't run. These people don't necessarily get recognition for what they do but are indispensable. She had some problems with such people but benefits too with this configuration in her chart.

She herself was definitely a key person who did not always get recognition (Vertex people do not get the recognition that Midheaven people do) for the indispensable services she supplied.

Example Five

This woman had a difficult start in life. Her father died when she was quite young and her mother used her as a kind of Cinderella housekeeper for the family. Needless to say, the atmosphere was unhappy and there was much fighting in the home (Mars in fourth opposition Midheaven, as well as Venus ruling the fourth square Midheaven, and Mercury square Midheaven).

When she left home it was to get away from this unhappiness, never realizing that she would walk right into another situation almost as bad. She married and she and her husband never got along. There were constant arguments; in fact, everyone knew (Midheaven) that she was unhappily married (Venus, Mercury-Midheaven, Mars T-Cross in her horoscope). She held various jobs off and on, most of which were clerical (Mercury) but one which involved research (Pluto trine Midheaven).

Despite the poor background, this woman has met some prominent, prestigious, and well-off people (Sun sextile Midheaven and Jupiter parallel Midheaven) who have tried to help her. Even though the unhappy marriage situation continued for almost 30 years, she managed to find some solace in her outside-the-home impersonal contacts (Midheaven) and the fact that people were generous with her.

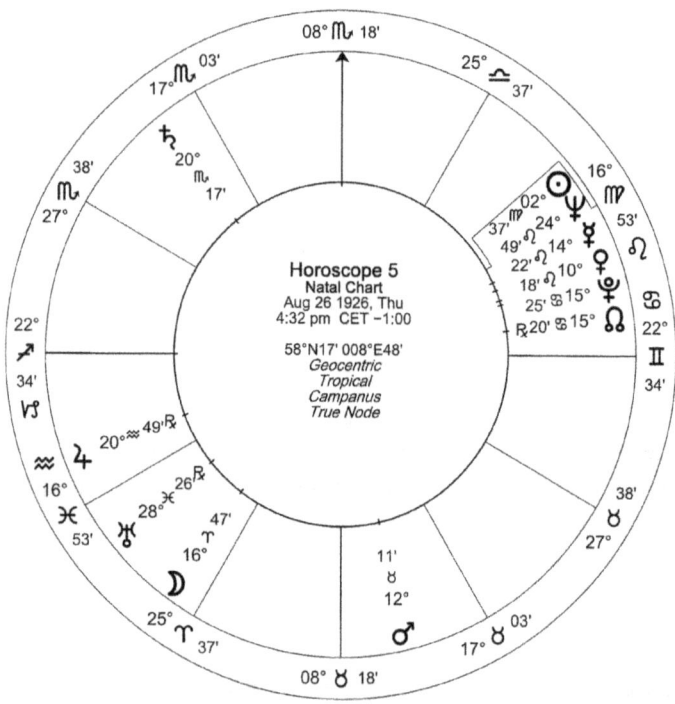

Uranus square Ascendant made her sometimes act contrary to her own best interests when it came to money. She never had much money and depended on the income her husband made, which wasn't adequate.

She has a positive, cheerful, breezy personality (Sagittarius with Moon trine from Aries) with a bright talkative style (Mercury trine from Leo). One would not guess her dissatisfaction and depression beneath the Ascendant veneer. She was helped in financial ways by women associates, too (Moon trine Ascendant from the second house).

Her social life was largely formed through business and outside-the-home interests (Venus square Midheaven) and served as a kind of sublimation for her emotionally unhappy marriage (Mars-Venus-Midheaven contact). Her husband did support her for most of the 30 years (Sun sextile Midheaven) of marriage. She has an interest in astrology and has built a slight reputation as a professional, but with some problems (Neptune contraparallel Midheaven).

Mercury-Venus conjunct the Vertex (14 Leo 04) and Mars and Saturn square it in fixed signs make the emotionally frustrating "role" she played for 30 years in her marriage appear rather fated and beyond her control (Vertex). Fixed crosses like this tend to remain in situations long after they should.

Example Six

This woman projects both an emotional quality and aggressiveness. Tears alternate with loud purposeful commands when she gets excited (Mars in Pisces conjunction Ascendant). She is not averse to a few curse words either (Mars-Ascendant)—a little like a first sergeant.

She is restless and much more active than you would expect a double Taurus to be (Mars-Uranus rising in Pisces). She impresses you almost immediately with her possessiveness and acquisitiveness (Moon in Taurus contraparallel Ascendant from the second house). Collecting "things" is important to her. She seems rather nervously talkative and flirtatious (Uranus conjunction Venus rising) at times.

She doesn't really have a career, but she has worked as a receptionist-helper to a chiropractor and other medical people (Neptune trine Midheaven from the sixth house and Moon close quincunx from the second house of money, ruling the sixth). She has also worked for and had much contact with psychiatrists and psychologists.

The latter was in connection with her son who had a ner-

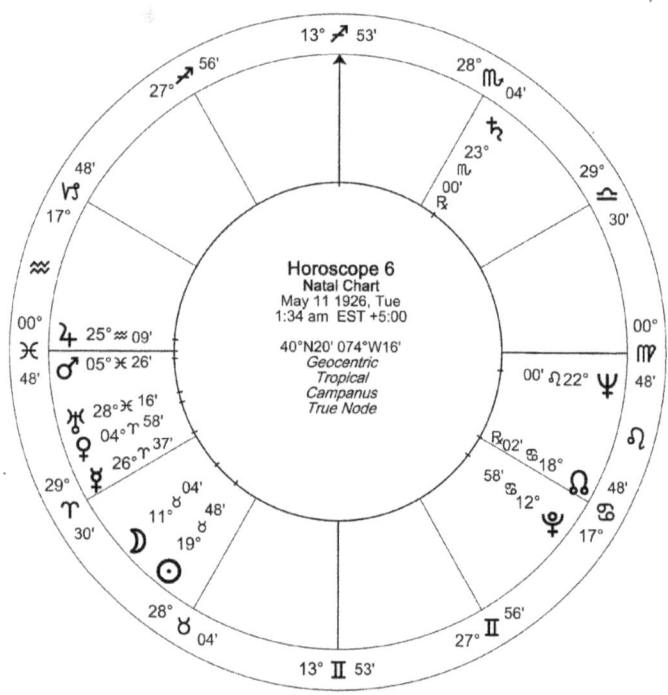

vous breakdown and had been under a psychologist's care for some time before the illness (Pluto contraparallel Midheaven). She keeps a link with these doctors because of her son's problem (Pluto aspects from late in the fifth house).

She had been a sergeant in the army during the war and is interested in physical therapy through her work (Mars square Midheaven). She seems energetic and can swing a hammer along with the best carpenters. She builds things and has an artistic talent that shows mostly in sculpture and three-dimensional work (Mars in a water sign and Venus conjunct Uranus rising). Had the Midheaven been a few degrees within orb of a trine to Venus in the first house she might have made art her career. As it is, it simply remains a talent that she enjoys.

Between the efforts of her husband and herself they have been able to accumulate a little real estate which is shown by Saturn (ruling real estate) in the eighth house, a singleton, trine rising Uranus and square Neptune-Jupiter.

There are other things in this chart that would give deeper insight into the conditions of her marriage and her life. But since we are concentrating on the meanings and importance of angles in the life pattern, I do not think it advisable to expand further.

It is obvious, of course, that in this chart with the Sun involved in a fixed T-Cross with Saturn, Neptune and Jupiter that she would have her problems with men (among other things). Also, her first house is a big one with many planets in it, so that her personality projection is a complex one when also combined with aspects to the Ascendant.

Example Seven

This is the horoscope of a woman who is married and has five children. She also runs a successful answering service in the little town where she lives. Her career is beautifully indicated by Mercury opposition the Midheaven (she runs the business out of her home). Her mother has been most helpful to her in this business which is clearly shown by Pluto (Mother) trine the Midheaven. She has also been involved in selling antiques with the help of her husband (Saturn sextile Midheaven from the seventh house), and at one time was in partnership with someone else selling antiques.

Her manner is soft and womanly (Cancer Ascendant), but she has a gaze that seems to look beneath the surface (Pluto rising). She also has a sunny warmth and magnanimity which comes through the Sun sextile the Ascendant. She likes to do things in a big way.

Running the answering service in her home has its problems (Mercury opposition Midheaven) because she hires people to work answering phones and she also does some of the work herself. With five children and a mother living at home, it can be rather busy.

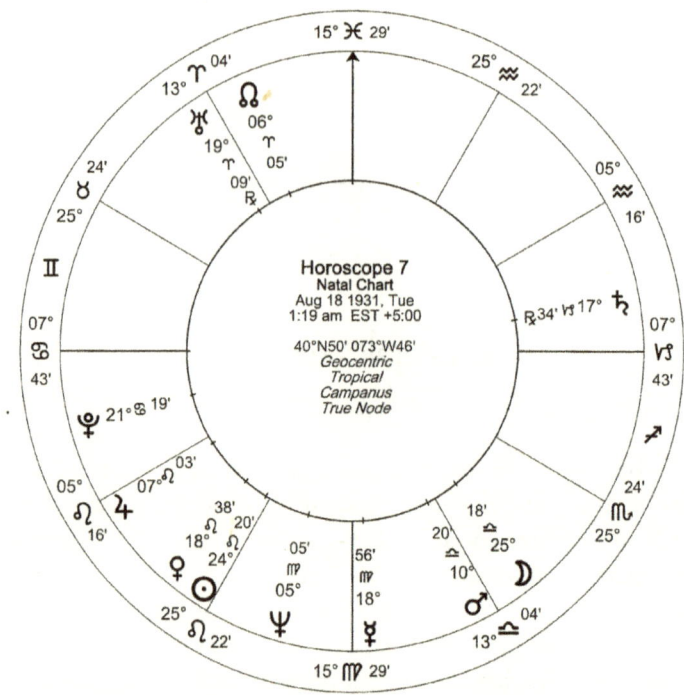

Neptune rules her Midheaven, is in her third house and, along with the Sun, aspects her Ascendant from the third house. The business she runs is a third house kind of activity. The Pisces-Neptune describes being a kind of "stand-in" or substitute for answering people's phones (Neptune rules pseudonyms, phonies, and substitutes). The person who answers the phone takes the place of one who isn't there (Neptune)—acting a part.

Her Sun is square the Vertex at 25 Scorpio 20 from the cusp of the third to the cusp of the sixth house. The service she performs is a local one and in a way involves her with large groups of people (the public) over which she has little or no control (Vertex). She is compelled to take messages and listen to people's requests and this is somehow very fated and karmic for her.

Example Eight

This is the chart of a man who was married to a woman for 28 years. They lived an exceedingly secluded existence except for their mutual jobs.

She was successful in the fashion and art fields and their lives mostly revolved around her hours and her needs since she made most of the income. The man's subservience to her schedule, such as getting up at five o'clock in the morning to drive her to the train, seems well depicted by Moon conjunction Mars in the twelfth opposition Uranus square the Midheaven. She was very antisocial and extremely independent (also described by Moon-Uranus-Midheaven).

When his chart was rectified, it was hard to understand why he would have Venus in the tenth and ruling the Midheaven since it did not seem to describe his career. It wasn't until I realized how important his wife's artistic career was in their lives that I could see what a high regard he had for her ambitions and accomplishments. His future depended on her successes.

Because he came from an exceedingly poor background, she seemed like a rich accomplished American in his eyes. As it

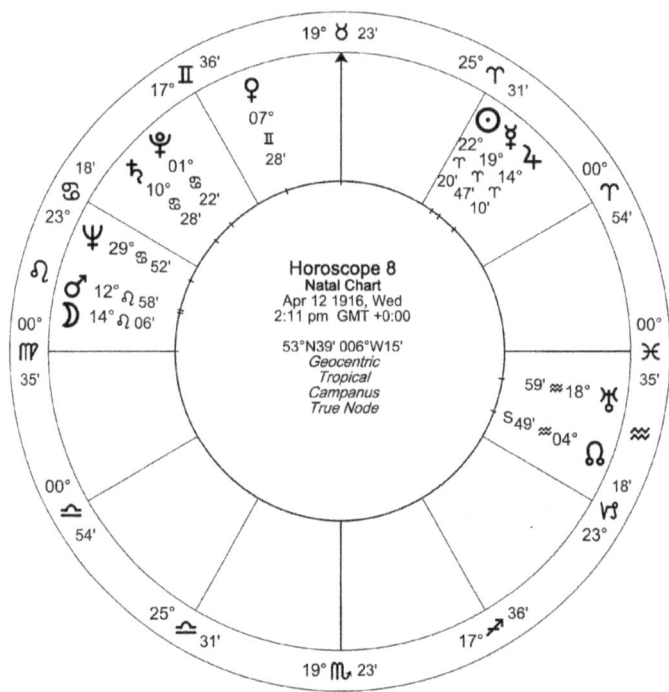

turned out, he did inherit money from her when she died (Sun trine Ascendant from the eighth house, Jupiter trine Moon from the eighth house).

He had owned and operated an electrical business (Uranus square Midheaven) that was fairly successful but very hectic and a bit unreliable as to income. Also, it interfered with her activities, so he eventually gave it up. He then went to work for a large electric cable company (again Uranian).

With Venus square the Ascendant he is publicly well liked and was at heart much more sociable than his wife; in fact, so much so that it interfered with business at times. He had emigrated from another country, and improved conditions and finances were the result (Sun trine the Ascendant from late in the eighth house, which has some ninth house influence). He projected a naturally sunny disposition, although he could be a bit shy at times (Sun trine Virgo Ascendant).

There was something strangely private about his marriage. His wife had been deserted by her parents, and she had a difficult start in life with unfortunate experiences. They did not agree on social life, so he agreed to spend most of their time alone together. With Neptune ruling the seventh house of marriage and in the twelfth house opposition the Vertex (28 Capricorn 56), their relationship was probably very fated and something they had to live out together. The Sun being square Neptune is also square the Vertex, and so his moving from one country to another to pursue his vital interests (Sun) was also a very fated matter beyond his control.

Again, the Sun has acted as a supreme benefic, being in aspect to two angles—the Ascendant and Vertex. From a poor beginning he rose to fair prominence and affluence.

Example Nine

This is the chart of a woman who had a driving ambition to be a playwright and worked at it from the time she was nine years old. The strong conjunction of Sun in Taurus with Mars square the Ascendant, and Neptune opposition Ascendant, made her a fanatic about this for many years. There always seemed to be some conflict between her marriage obligations (Neptune in the seventh) and her writing, but she persevered.

When you first meet her, she seems to have a rather aloof manner, detached in a sort of nebulous way (Neptune opposition end of Capricorn, mostly Aquarius first house). Yet she projects an energetic good humor (Sun-Mars square Ascendant) and always appears to be going somewhere with a purpose.

In order to be successful as a playwright, or as any writer for that matter, you naturally have to be published, which means having good ninth house connections. To be recognized by the public you should have aspects of Moon to Midheaven and also possibly Jupiter. After numerous attempts to publish without success, she began to be discouraged—Pluto, ruler of the ninth house is contraparallel the Midheaven. Not only is the planet a malefic but the aspect is difficult as well. Also, she has no helpful

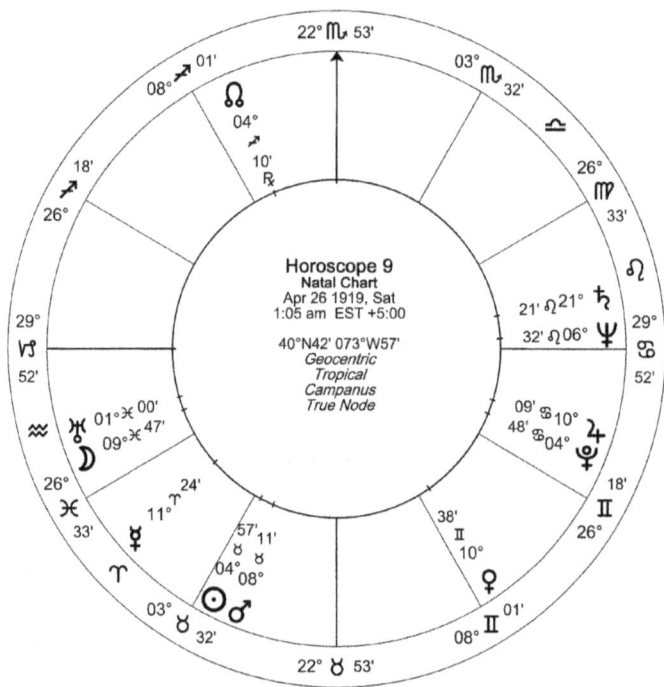

contacts of Moon and Jupiter to her Midheaven. After a period of great frustration (fixed crosses feel great frustration at times) she began to be more and more interested in a religious group.\

The chart as a whole shows a need to be one-pointedly dedicated to something or someone. She did, in the beginning, look for God in a man, her husband (Sun-Mars square Neptune in the seventh house). But of course this did not work, and her marriage was a source of unhappiness because her husband was a dependent type who had difficulty making a living (Neptune and Saturn square Midheaven from the seventh house).

She finally joined the religious group and became dedicated to their service in the same one-pointed way she had worked at her writing. The marriage still exists but the writing has stopped. It is a tragic story of one who did not have the necessary benefic influences to her Midheaven to bring her work out into the open.

She has Sun square Ascendant and her husband comes from a socially elevated background and does receive help from his family. Also, her talent as a writer made it possible for her to work at home writing synopses of books she read for possible television or movie production.

She also has Sun trine Vertex (1 Virgo 28) and has been brought into contact with key men in special group (Vertex) situations. The Sun contacting both the Ascendant and Vertex has certainly helped her throughout her life. Yet when you weigh this against Neptune afflicting both Midheaven and Ascendant, Pluto afflicting both Midheaven and Ascendant, and Saturn afflicting Midheaven, the benefit from the Sun seems to pale.

Example Ten

This is the horoscope of a man who was in the investment field. People consulted him about buying stocks (a seventh house Moon often indicates that "others" come to consult an individual, and in this case the Moon influences the eighth house on the "hidden" side). Note that Saturn in the tenth house ruling his eighth also emphasizes the financial or investment field.

He was very smooth in handling others and quite dependent on their cooperation (Venus in the seventh ruling his Ascendant. Also, the Pluto-Mars-Venus-Midheaven planetary picture is descriptive of a clever salesman with Mars aspecting from the speculative fifth house).

He invested heavily in a railroad stock and held the important position of chairman of the board of directors, which was a job with much prestige and responsibility (Sun/Jupiter = Midheaven, as well as Saturn conjunct Midheaven). This is a splendid example of Midpoints involving the Midheaven as the central axis and how it affected the career.

At one point he was so anxious to get others to invest in the railroad to reinforce his own position that he persuaded them to

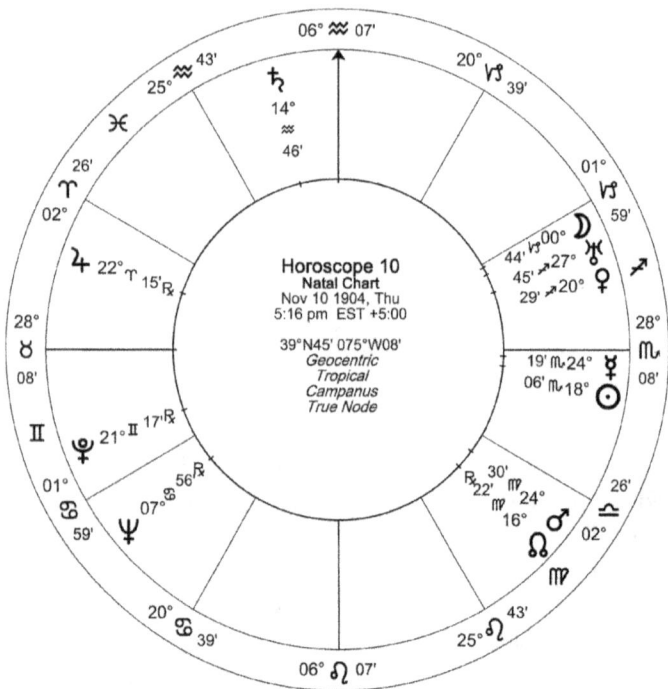

back the railroad even though he knew it was going bankrupt (Pluto-Venus-Midheaven is not always straightforward). With Sun, Moon, and Jupiter contacting the Midheaven, he got away with his own skin but left a lot of other people holding the bag.

Example Eleven

This is a success story of a man who went to a new country with virtually no money and built up a substantial jewelry business through his own drive and initiative (The jewelry business is shown by Jupiter square Midheaven and Venus sesquiquadrate Midheaven and the purposeful drive by Mars opposition Midheaven). In his business he not only designs jewelry (Uranus/Mercury = Midheaven = inventive thinking) but also deals with much complicated machinery (Uranus/Mars = Midheaven).

He has two of the necessary benefic aspects to make an impact on the world around him—Moon parallel Midheaven and Ascendant/Sun = Midheaven. Of course Uranus square the Midheaven indicates some sudden changes and nerve-wracking ups and downs. Also, with Mars opposition Midheaven, he has thrown most of his energies into the business, which did not leave much left over for anything else.

You will note too that he has the third benefic, Jupiter, square Midheaven. With all the benefics contacting his Midheaven he has made a tremendous success of a venture that started out with nothing.

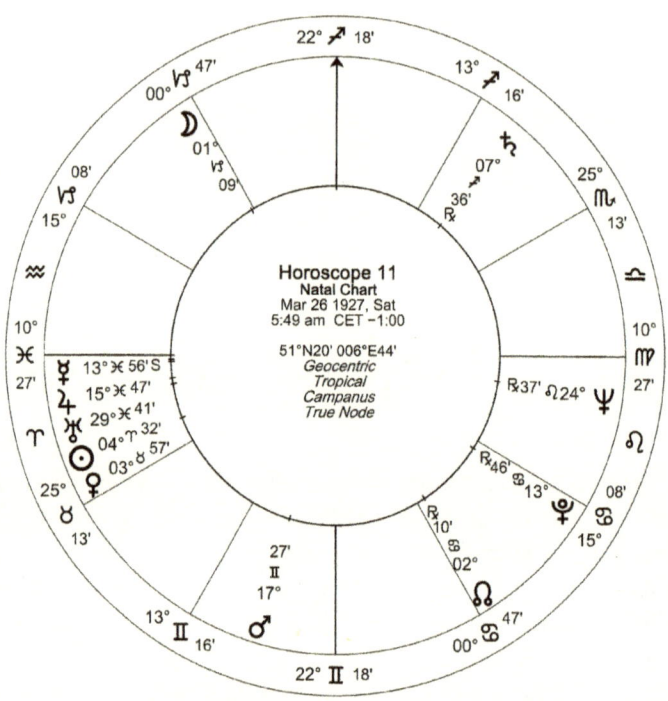

Example Twelve

This is the chart of a man who was in the investment field as a technical analyst. He went into the field when he was very young. A college graduate with high honors, he was determined to be a success.

He worked very long hours trying to establish his own business (Ascendant/Saturn = Midheaven) and damaged his health to some extent doing this. At one point he had an unreliable partner, an alcoholic (Neptune square Midheaven from the seventh house) who almost ruined the business him.

He began to make impressions on people with his reliable financial forecasts (constructive side of Neptune to Sagittarius Midheaven). But his success story is really shown by Moon trine Midheaven, Venus trine Midheaven, Jupiter semisquare Midheaven and the two benefic midpoint pictures Midheaven/Sun = Ascendant and Moon/Ascendant = Sun. The latter is more personal in nature and it should be said that this man's personal life is so intertwined with his business interests it is almost impossible to separate them. This is indicated by the combined Midheaven-Ascendant planetary picture of Midheaven/Sun = Ascendant. He has all four benefics to the Midheaven and this

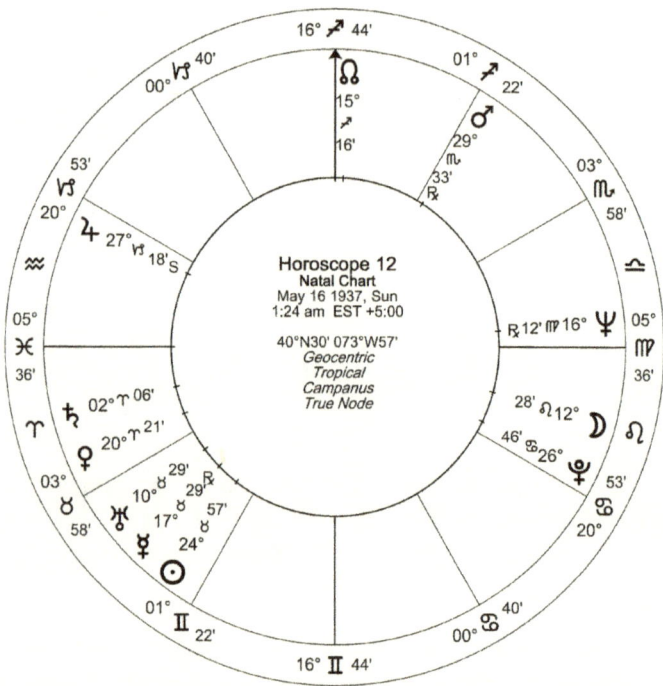

assured his eventual rise to the top. He was also very fortunate in the women who helped him with much of the hard work involved in getting a business off the ground (Moon trine Midheaven from the sixth house).

Example Thirteen

This is the chart of a professional astrologer. This profession is usually shown by either Neptune or Uranus involved with the Midheaven. In this case both planets are involved: Neptune is trine Midheaven and Uranus is sextile. He also has three planetary pictures involving midpoints and the Midheaven: Midheaven/Saturn = Neptune, Neptune/Uranus = Saturn/Midheaven, and Uranus/Ascendant = Midheaven/Moon.

He is very well known, which the last picture indicates by the Moon's contact to Midheaven. Saturn involved with the Midheaven picture shows the responsibility he carries in connection with clients who consult him (Saturn from the eleventh.) This is another case where the Ascendant and Midheaven are combined in a midpoint picture and this shows the inextricable intertwining of personal and public life, which is very true in his case.

He is a very social being; indeed, both lights are ruled by Venus and Venus is sextile Ascendant and trine his Moon. Also, he has two midpoint pictures with Venus to his Ascendant—Moon/Ascendant = Venus and Venus/Jupiter = Sun = Ascendant.

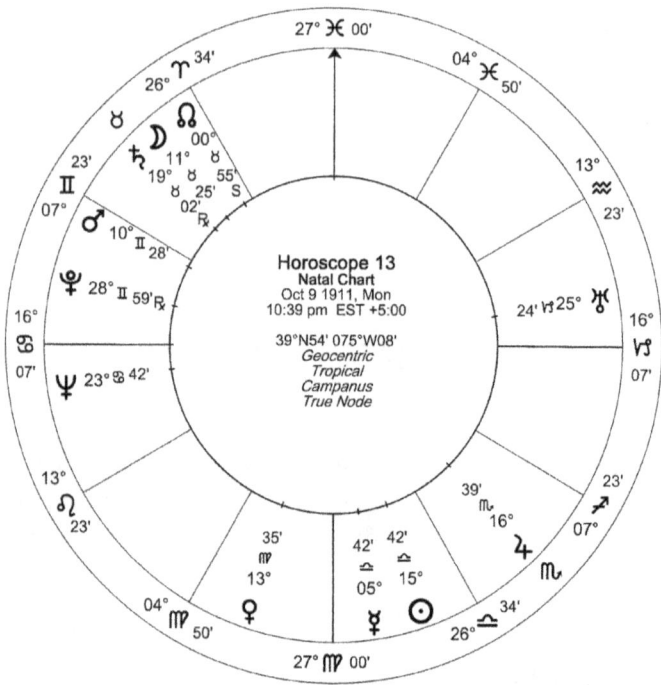

Although he is well known, he has had financial conflicts most of his life (Sun square his Ascendant). The Sun brought prominent men into his personal life and some affluence, yet he has inner conflicts about how to handle finances. He does a great deal of writing, shown by Mercury parallel Midheaven and Sun/Midheaven = Mercury, and is fairly aggressive with ideas (Mars in Gemini parallel Ascendant, Mars/Sun = Midheaven, and Mars/Ascendant = Midheaven).

Example Fourteen, Henry Kissinger

A time of 5:30 am was given in the birth records for this horoscope which gives a 22 Aquarius Midheaven and 25 Gemini Ascendant. However, since Mr. Kissinger gave 6:00 am as the accurate birth time. The 6:00 am chart was chosen as being closer to the right time through "common sense" rectification.

In the earlier chart the Sun would not aspect the Midheaven, and in view of his constant dealings with prominent people (Sun) behind the scenes (twelfth house), the Sun square Midheaven in the later chart seems more appropriate.

Then too, the earlier chart would give him late Gemini conjunction an angular Mars, which certainly would make him an aggressive and sometimes tactless arguer. Mr. Kissinger seems to have more subtle finesse than this would indicate—much more described by the softer Cancer rising with Mars back in the twelfth house but still conjunction Ascendant (he is very physically active and gets around a great deal).

With Pluto rising close to the Ascendant this would give him a more penetrating psychological perspicacity, which he certainly has. Venus within five degrees of a sextile to the later

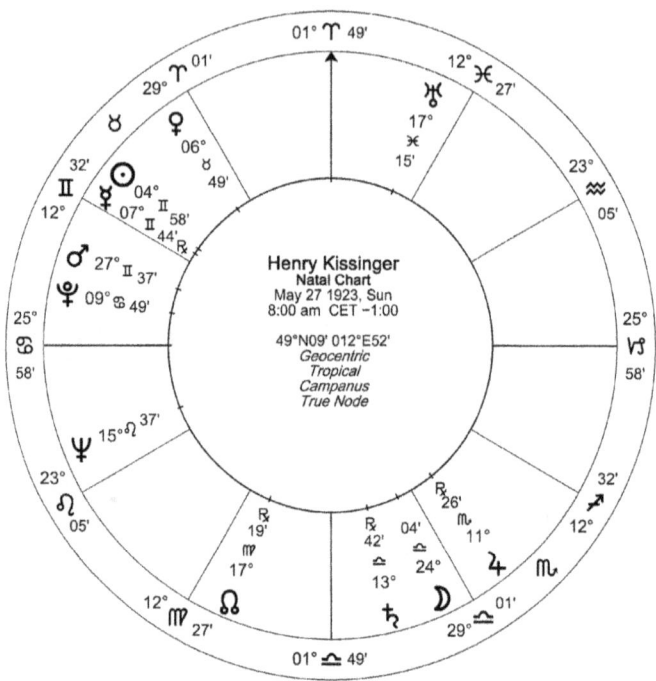

Ascendant gives the sense of decorum and suaveness apparent in his personality projection.

It should be noted that Uranus falls late in the tenth house, casting its influence in both the tenth and eleventh houses. The variety of people he deals with at a very hectic pace is not only avocational-social like the eleventh house but the career-focused tenth house as well.

Before his marriage he had a reputation for being quite a man with the ladies (shown by Mars conjunction Ascendant trine Moon in the fifth house). Mercury square the Midheaven as well as the Sun would indicate a certain amount of public speaking and writing, which is also true.

At the time that Mr. Kissinger was threatened with becoming involved with the Watergate situation he gave more evidence that his rising sign would certainly be a water sign. He apparently had had a very heavy traveling schedule and was over-tired at the time and when the reporters began asking accusatory questions the tears came to his eyes in apparent frustration. The liquidity of tears does not occur too easily with air signs rising so this is another indication of the validity of a Cancer Ascendant in his horoscope.

Example Fifteen, L. Edward Johndro

Most people who know about Johndro think of him as an astrologer who wrote books, which was true. However, he was also a radio engineer who taught his subject and advised prominent business people about their stock investments.

Being an astrologer and writer-teacher is clearly shown by Mercury and Neptune aspecting his Midheaven (and Sun in the third house). The prominent men he advised are probably shown by his Sun opposite Midheaven and Jupiter square it (Jupiter is the planet dealing with high finance). Advising people about their investments could also be shown by his Moon sextile Midheaven from the eighth house.

One of the interesting and little known facts about Johndro's life is that he had a very important silent partnership with another astrologer, Kenneth Brown, for 15 years. With Neptune-Saturn square his Sun, opposition his Ascendant and square his Midheaven, he had a morbid fear of direct contact with people. Saturn is on the "hidden side" of his seventh house, describing the silent partner, and Neptune is also a secretive planet. Mr. Brown did most of the direct consulting, although Johndro did the technical work. They never met but carried on the entire

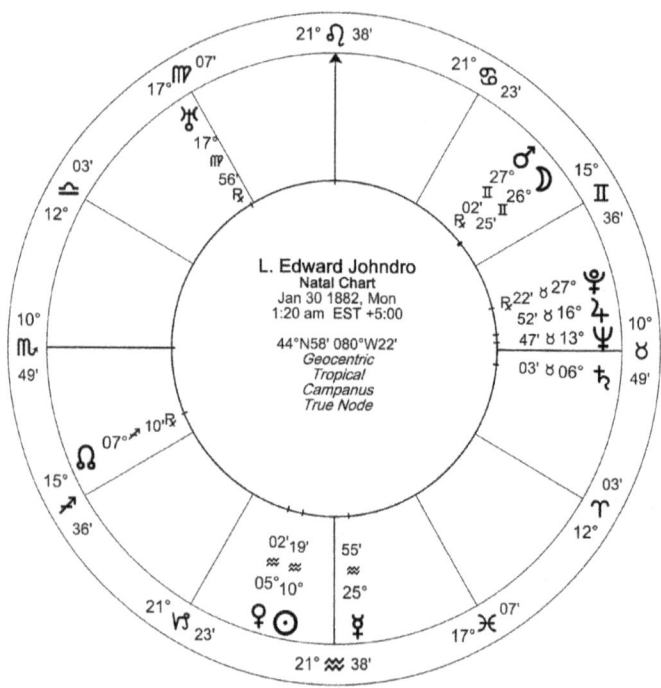

business relationship through correspondence (third house Sun rules the tenth house). His dislike of getting involved with people probably drove him to accept this partnership, which worked very well for them both.

Although he was a recluse and had a reticent personality, he had a healthy opinion of himself and did not like to share his knowledge. He had a way of writing over the heads of his colleagues and expected to be exceptionally well paid for anything he did. Expecting much from others could also be Jupiter in the seventh opposite Ascendant and square Sun.

He would probably have preferred to be a loner, yet with three planets plus Saturn on the seventh house side, partners were very important to him, including his marriage of long standing. We must also remember that Pluto, ruler of his Ascendant, is in the seventh house.

Perhaps one of the reasons stocks and commodities played an important role in his life was because he had Moon conjunct Vertex (20 Gemini 08) in the eighth house and Mercury trine Vertex ruling the eighth house. During his life he partly supported himself by playing the stock and commodity markets.

Chart Data

Chart	Given Time	Rectified Time	Rectifiers
1	9:00 pm EST	9:39:34	Charles and Vivia Jayne
2	11:32 am EST	Not rectified	
3	6:00 am GMT	7:53	Charles and Vivia Jayne
4	3:00 am EST	4:28	Charles Jayne
5	5:00 pm CET	4:32	Charles Jayne
6	2:00-4:00 am EST	1:34	Charles and Vivia Jayne
7	2:00-3:00 am EST	1:19	Charles Jayne
8	2:30 pm GMT	2:11	Charles and Vivia Jayne
9	1:00 am EST	1:05	Charles Jayne
10	5:25 pm EST	5:16	Charles Jayne
11	6:00 am CET	5:49	Charles Jayne
12	2:00-3:00 am EST	1:24	Charles and Vivia Jayne
13	10:53 pm EST	10:39:30	Eleanor Hesseltine
14	5:30 am CET (Birth Record)	Unrectified	
	6:00 am CET (By native to Julie Eisenhower)		Used 6:00 am
15	Unknown	1:20 am EST	L. Edward Johndro